FAULT LINES

Gary Beck

This publication is a creative work protected in full by all applicable copyright laws, as well as by misappropriation, trade secret, unfair competition, and other applicable laws. No part of this book may be reproduced or transmitted in any manner without written permission from Winter Goose Publishing, except in the case of brief quotations embodied in critical articles or reviews. All rights reserved.

Winter Goose Publishing
45 Lafayette Road #114
North Hampton, NH 03862

www.wintergoosepublishing.com
Contact Information: info@wintergoosepublishing.com

Fault Lines

COPYRIGHT © 2016 by Gary Beck

First Edition, October 2016

Cover Design by Winter Goose Publishing
Typesetting by Odyssey Books

ISBN: 978-1-941058-55-8

Published in the United States of America

To Rhonda McClam
Brave, bright, talented, creative,
determined to forge a better life

With love and admiration,
Gary Beck

Bien souvent j'ai plané si haut
Si haut qu'adieu toutes les chose

"Les Collines"—Guillaume Apollinaire

CONTENTS

Symphony of the City	1
Perilous Clime	2
The Information Age	3
Homo Homini Lupus	4
State of the Union	6
School Days	11
Advanced Warfare	13
Ominous Signs	14
Dumbing Down	15
The Spoils of War	16
Lost in the Land of Plenty	26
Make the World Safe For . . .	27
Equilibrium	28
Fueling Lunacy	30
Wishful Thinking	32
Battlefield	33
Inequality	36
American Intervals	38
The Long View	40
Elegy to The Child Soldier	42
Do We Get What We Pay For?	45
Bombs Bursting in Iraq	46
Iraq Dilemma	48
Biofuel Confusion	50
Running Interference	55

Depredation	56
Reality Check	57
Questions of War	58
Role Reversals	60
The Democratic System	61
Rules of Engagement	62
Danger Sign	63
Desertion, or Treason?	64
Brief Dreams	67
Mass Communication	68
Cycle of Destruction	69
High Policy	70
Urban Sorrow	71
Iraqi Blues	72
Serenity	73
Learning Experience	74
Harsh Reality	75
Compliance	76
Soldier's Pay	77
Bureaucratic Priorities	79
Gifts of Man	80
Ode to Automatic Weaponry	81
Climate Change	82
Grudge	83
Planned Obsolescence	84
All the News	85
Deep Sixed	86

Brief Bereavement	87
Beaten Down	88
Ex-President	89
Winter of Discontent	90
Swan Song	91
Super Highway	92
Harvest	93
Overwhelmed	94
Vox Populi	95
Darwinism	96
Attrition	97
American Myths	98
Lost Souls	99
Shock Treatment	100
Urban Expansion	101
Deceptive Aim	102
Shopping Spree	103
Demented Species	104
Récherché le Chose Perdue	105
Russian Visit, 1903	106
Last Chance	107
The Counting of the Homeless	108
Altogether Dreamless	109
You Can't Go Home Again	110
No Salvation	111
Victims of the Past	112
Pedestrian Traffic	113

Waste Not	114
Munich in the Mist	115
Two Dirges	116
Sacrifice	117
Redeemed	118
Guilt	119
No Forgiveness	120
Three Rueful Songs	121
Finis	122
About the Author	124

Symphony of the City

Discordant orchestra
rent by untuned instruments,
the underlying hum of engines
sound the theme of endless din.
The clack of workmen moving pipes,
the bumpthump of delivery trucks,
the unrythmic thud of hammer,
the voices of children
cavorting in the playground
serenade the senses,
varied sensual sounds
interrupted by crash and bang,
handymen, repair crews,
horn-blowing motorists
aspiring to be soloists,
daytime throb of labor.
Nighttime crack of gunfire,
shrieks and howls
of citizens in torment
under constant assault,
reveal the melody
of your anguished composition.

Perilous Clime

Unlike plagues of eld,
nomadic hordes
temporarily destroying
tribes, cities, nations
that may not have recovered,
but allowed continuation
of civilization,
consistent devouring
of the fruits of earth,
outpouring of unnatural elements
poisoning the finite supply
of air, water, food,
may combine to prevent
sufficient resources
for arks of survival.

The Information Age

In days of old
access to communication
was restricted to oral,
tongues mostly held
because the wrong words
could lead to loss of heads.
There was limited chatter
restricted to exchanges
of vital information
useful for survival.
Now everywhere we go
people are attached
to hi-tech cell phones.
The endless flow of babble
dominates the airwaves,
ultimately threatening
the continued existence
of serious transmissions.

Homo Homini Lupus

In the lowlands of Mozambique
an old technology of war,
the child soldier, swept Africa
and later the rest of the world.
Immature killing machines
sliced their way through villages
bringing fire and destruction
to the innocent in their path.

Warlords seeking plunder
find children the perfect weapon:
fearless, manipulable,
they are an endless supply.

Once young killers are unleashed
they murder relentlessly,
unconcerned with hearts and minds,
not needing popular support,
just approval from their masters
for carrying out orders
to commit bloody massacres.

They are not hallowed warriors
respected by those they protect.
They will have no parades.
No trumpets will sing their praises.
They will be remembered,
with pity or hatred.

STATE OF THE UNION

My fellow citizens.
I fear the future
of our bountiful nation
is in imminent danger
of survival.

The nuclear family
has been supplanted by
the dysfunctional family,
dumbing our children.

Many public schools,
except for the privileged,
are academies of failure
creating purposeless legions
of disaffected youth, denied,
by a moribund system,
a sense of achievement,
so they repay us daily
with anger and madness
to punish our neglect.

We can only wonder
if the schools are well-meaning.

In our once bountiful nation,
with more churches and sects
than any other nation,
religion in all its forms
will not suffice
to avert calamity.

Lost wars haunt our land.
The war on crime,
drugs, poverty,
other crusades
designed to deceive
our trusting people
that our government
of, by, for, etc.,
is concerned with our well-being.

We can only wonder
who is well-meaning.

In our struggling nation
corporations rush abroad,
abandoning the origins
that allowed enrichment,
until swollen with appetite
for endless profit
they renounce the people
who nourished them,
leaving the service sector

beckoning our youth
to diminishing comforts.

Yet we act surprised
when rejected offspring
erupt in tragic violence,
while custodians of tomorrow,
failing in their duty,
are richly rewarded.

We can only wonder
how we remain well-meaning.

In our besieged nation
the air becomes more toxic,
the water more tainted,
the food supply more tasteless
in a land divided,
at peril as never before
of unavoidable conflict
between children of endurance
and heirs of privilege,
whose only catechism
is "after us, the deluge."

The wielders of power
slyly disassembled
the blue collar working class
whose sons and daughters

lost tools of resistance
to endless abuses
by the lords of profit.

We can only wonder
how long we will be well-meaning.

In our declining nation
more hated than feared abroad,
more confused than certain at home,
illegal hordes of aliens
swarm our porous borders,
encouraged by political correctness
allowing amateur architects
to construct the tower of Babel,
until the clamor of foreign tongues
frays lines of communication
between established communities,
legitimate colonists, illicit intruders.

And the lords of profit
securely perched
above turbulence
gloat in satisfaction
as we are distracted
by mindless diversions,
TV, sports, electronic amusements
that allow no cognition
of long-term danger.

Detached from issues of reality
we are easily discarded.

My fellow citizens.
The state of the union is threatened
and we can only wonder
if it is too late for well-meaning.

SCHOOL DAYS

High schools in America
have at least several loners
seething with resentment,
alienated for years
by insensitive peers.

Colleges in America
have multiple loners
transformed by rage
into creatures of hate,
ready to detonate.

When an individual
or group finally explodes
into extreme violence,
the survivors are dazed,
the public is amazed.

This is what we allowed
building an insane system
esteeming brawn over brains,
where athletes are adored
and thinkers are ignored.

It shouldn't be a surprise
when gunfire erupts
across a hallowed campus,
the weak striking back
for the attention they lack.

ADVANCED WARFARE

In Internet chatrooms,
where young radicals gather,
the fight for hearts and minds
is being won by extremists
who misuse Islam
to persuade the weak
that suicide bombing is righteous,
glorifying attackers,
proclaiming them martyrs.
The speed of Internet transmission
from intention to execution
compels us to understand
that we must quickly change
the values of young radicals,
or risk electronic recruitment
to paths of detonation.

Ominous Signs

Disturbing predictions,
calamities striking
a recumbent land,
too easily ignored
by ignorant people
concerned with comforts,
not the future of the nation.

The ministers of greed
have educated us
to accept without thinking
loss of the war on drugs,
loss of the war on poverty,
all the other lost wars,
preparing us to accept
loss of the war on terror.

Dumbing Down

The biofuel industry
though relatively recent
wants to make a profit
like other industries
and farmers in Italy
hoping to get rich quick
started growing rapeseed weed
instead of wheat for pasta.

Perhaps the oil industry
will allow consumers
to start using biofuels
before oil is exhausted,
but no one with intelligence
expects that to happen.

So alternative energy,
not much cheaper than oil,
will motivate greedy farmers
to stop growing our food supply
and we may get hungry,
but our cars will keep running.

The Spoils of War

The United States of America
never fought a war of self-defense,
but inherited a tradition
from European forebears
to fight for land, resources,
other valuables.
As industry developed
we resorted to armed conflict
for our share of markets,
foreign and domestic.

We always claimed a righteous cause,
our masters cynically knowing
the way to rouse the nation's wrath
against the selected enemy.

After the guns fell silent
the dead were quickly forgotten,
except by family and friends.
The wounded soon were neglected,
except by family and friends,
until they also lost interest.
Many clever ex-soldiers
quickly sought public office,
while memories of their triumphs
were convertible to rewards.

Most soldiers who survived
our general's leadership
and hostile actions of our foes,
rapidly returned to civilian life
with no transition from the battlefield
and were easily abandoned
by once supportive leaders,
because they were no longer needed,
until World War II began,
when we became a global player.

Then the lords of profit remembered
the threat of the bonus marchers,
who after World War I were promised
rich rewards for their sacrifices,
which were conveniently forgotten.

So betrayed veterans marched
on Washington DC, demanding
government keep its pledge.
Instead they met Douglas MacArthur,
who crushed their hopes with troops and tanks.

And the lords of profit realized
that the legions had seen a bigger world
than the trenches of World War I
and would not be as easily duped
as veterans of earlier wars,
they devised a plan

to tempt the returning legions
with promotion to middle class,
made possible by education
with the GI Bill of Rights.

And the veterans flourished.
Newly armed with higher incomes
they joined the consumer crusade
with ever-growing fervor,
acquired goods and services,
endorsing the hallowed principle
of frequency of replacement,
manipulated by TV
accepting blindly
they were what they bought.

The children of this nouveau class,
wallowing in luxuries
unimagined in ages past,
were effortlessly deceived
into expecting entitlements,
were expertly deluded
by the unexpected success
of the Civil Rights Movement,
America's last noble cause,
into believing they mattered.

Then the children of comfort
freed from toil in the fields,

rescued from crush of factories,
turned attention to Vietnam
with righteous indignation,
protested the evils of war,
refusing to join the legions
manned by sons of the poor,
sent to Asian jungles
with the banner of democracy.

When our bitterest war ended,
the children of comfort rejoiced,
celebrating their victory
over the forces of evil.
They could never imagine
that old ordnance was expended
so new ordnance could be purchased,
with enough new markets
so the war was no longer needed
and the lords of profit were glutted.

Still married to the Cold War
whose temperature fluctuated
with a corrosive agenda,
the lords of profit
chose technology
to replace manpower,
preferring low cost volunteers
to man hundred-million-dollar planes,
to man billion-dollar ships

and avoid the casualties
that always distressed America.

So eager volunteers
were permitted little wars
while the soviets were a threat,
but when they had a great fall
the lords of profit discovered
they no longer had an enemy
suitable for massive warfare,
and without massive warfare
they couldn't expend old ordnance
so they could sell new ordnance.

The lords of profit consulted
the oracle of Delphi,
Tiresias, the blind prophet,
Rosanna, the gypsy seeress,
the pentagon crystal ball,
and other intel sources
who were all in agreement
that an enemy was needed,
a monster, but not a real threat,
and they selected Saddam.

He qualified on every count.
He was a genuine monster,
a violent aggressor
of low moral rectitude,

oppressor of the weak,
addicted to torture,
and most conveniently
lacked long range aircraft,
lacked long range missiles,
and couldn't attack the USA.

We manufactured an issue,
Saddam's mad lust to obtain
Weapons of Mass Destruction.
If that wasn't pretext enough
to confuse our many skeptics,
his connection was discovered
to international terror,
so the generals and admirals
were allowed to unleash blitzkrieg.

Nothing was more satisfying
to the neglected military
then to overwhelm an enemy
with only moderate casualties,
which pleased the suspicious public,
who had feared defeat in the desert,
but now were given a victory
and gladly awarded a triumph
to the returning legions.
And the lords of profit were sated.

Satiation doesn't last long
when the coffers of industry,
the pockets of politicians,
the lunch pails of the working class
were not as full as they could be.
And these groups were useful
as the lords of profit continued
to plunder the land of its treasures,
breaking down sovereign borders,
sending jobs and capital abroad.

So the usual solution
of military adventure
with the usual restrictions
on collateral damage
caused the usual disasters.
And the usual scapegoats,
the defenseless military
became targets of public scorn.
And the men and women warfighters,
despite dedication to duty,
were sacrificed by the bureaucrats.

As we approached the twenty-first century
conditions economic and social
weren't positive domestically
and people were becoming restless,
for the lords of profit had removed
well-paying jobs with security

and cast many families adrift,
leaving little alternative
to accepting a lower lifestyle,
an end to their American dream.

Once again a war was needed
to divert our demanding people.
Once again we unleashed blitzkrieg
on appropriate recipients,
who we blamed for our many ills,
and they were rapidly defeated,
but spited us by resisting
our efforts at pacification,
knowing that we'd soon lose
our taste for prolonged battle.

Our politicians were divided.
Most of them had their own agenda.
Many spoke for special interests.
Many opposed the war in Iraq.
Many claimed to be patriots.
Many professed love for their country.
Yet the problems facing our nation
always seemed more difficult to solve
and a spirit of despair emerged
that further drained our resolution.

Then the voices of clamor were raised
by liberals and conservatives,
some demanding *Get out of Iraq*,
some demanding *Stay the course*,
and while our sons and daughters
were fighting fanatic enemies,
each day the media published
the list of our sons and daughters
killed or wounded in battle,
further breaking down public morale.

Our nation was further divided
into different citizen groups,
some who'd turn out to find a lost child,
others who'd stay home and complain.
Their differences grew more extreme.
Bitterness infected the people
further weakening their resolve
to deal with confusing issues
which delighted the breeders of sheep
in a world of ravenous wolves.

Then the lords of profit gloated
as dissension rendered the land,
preventing deeper inquiries
into the future of the land
menaced with so many dangers
that our people were in despair.
Those who still managed to care

were overwhelmed with the burdens
that an entire nation should share,
while threats of terror numbed the land.

Our legions stationed abroad,
strategically placed on foreign shores
to counter conceivable threats,
were unnoticed by the media,
unless they committed war crimes,
since the media were focused
on Iraq and Afghanistan,
distracting us with body counts
from domestic problems
that would insure our children's future.

We do not know what tomorrow brings,
but citizens who are hopeful
that the promise of America
is not beyond redemption
for those who believe in ideals
in the land where many strive
to better the lot of our people,
seek oracles of fulfillment
and must learn to be aware
of the dangers of false prophets.

Lost in the Land of Plenty

I live in a welfare hotel
and when the electricity
gets shut off again
in the room provided
by Homeless Services,
without the heater,
even with blankets,
it's freezing cold.

I hurry to dress
so I won't miss the bus
that will take me to school,
even though I hate it,
'cause they call me names
and make me sit in the back
with the other homeless kids.

But I try to ignore
how the teacher treats us,
how the other kids treat us,
'cause at least I'll be warm.

MAKE THE WORLD SAFE FOR . . .

I sit in comfort
in my Florida room
sipping iced tea,
watching flocks of birds,
cardinals, blue jays, robins,
colorful and diverse,
feeding, flirting, fighting,
providing delight,
while across my troubled land,
across the entire world
violence abounds,
domestic dispute,
felonious assault,
homicide, genocide,
constant terrorism
brought live in color,
twenty-four/seven,
courtesy of TV,
eager to fill the airwaves
with non-stop programming
of bloodshed and gore,
staple entertainment
for all nationalities,
regardless of persuasion,
united in viewing pleasure.

EQUILIBRIUM

For thousands of years
Europeans,
peasants or nobles,
cut down trees
indiscriminately.
Manicured forests
or man-made forests
are all that remain
to the old worlders,
now dependent
on diminishing fuel.

When chill reaches bone
and they shiver in darkness,
the hope of future comforts
will be exhausted.

For dozens of years
Americans,
regardless of class,
paved with concrete
indiscriminately.
Dwindling forests
or man-made forests
are all that remain
to the new worlders,

now dependent
on diminishing places
to absorb run-off.

When the water rises
and we shiver in darkness,
the hope of future comforts
will be exhausted.

Fueling Lunacy

Never before
in the course of human events
have we been close to eroding
the very fabric of nature
in a global crime
of commission and omission
as the lords of profit
market the means of destruction.

We pour endless miles of concrete
strangling the gasping Earth
struggling to endure assault
of poisons, toxins, chemicals,
that further reduce the supply
of breathable air,
drinkable water,
edible food.

The lords of profit maintain
a personal hoard that allows
respiration, hydration,
but they have forgotten
that we can only exist
a few minutes without breathing,
a few days without drinking.
We, the people, have also forgotten.

The rain forests are dwindling.
Desertification is spreading.
Much of the world goes hungry.
Disease consumes the poor.
Our planet is divided
into separate worlds
as we're misled into accepting
that we are not connected.

We construct crypts of entombment
while the wealthy flee
to privileged retreats,
deluded into believing
they will enjoy tomorrows
that may last a little longer
than most of the human race,
who have been betrayed
by the ministers of greed.

Wishful Thinking

The illusion of freedom
is righteously believed
by millions of Americans,
sheltered by consumer comforts,
who stir to reality
only when confronted
with shattering detonations
that fracture perceptions
that all may be well.

BATTLEFIELD

Our troops trudged
through Baghdad streets
fearing ambush
from hidden snipers,
roadside bombs,
other fatal means
that kill our men and women.
Yet soldiers and marines
obeyed orders,
went in harm's way
on dangerous Baghdad streets,
while our politicians,
generals, and admirals,
far from combat zones,
made decisions in safety
about hi-tech weapons
that may or may not be used
in future war
fought with hi-tech systems
that will promise victory.

As our troops patrolled
perilous Baghdad streets,
our leaders sat in comfort
behind the firing lines
imbibing vintage wines

like chateau generals
behind the firing lines
of World War I trenches,
so far from troops
they lost loyalty down,
an officer's obligation
to value troops
more than personal ambitions
even at cost of career,
an ethic forgotten
on the harsh road of advancement
that hardens the heart to concern
for the lives of weary troops,
who fought a different kind of war
than our generals would prefer.

In a democratic nation
founded on patriotic myths
it is difficult to accept
that corruption rules the land
and public personae
mask ulterior motives
leaving many citizens
without recourse
for liberty and justice.
So we submerge into TV,
neglect public duty
which encourages our leaders
to obey special interests

that build billion-dollar weapons
for admirals and generals
who overlook basic need
of personal body armor
for volunteers serving
in a distant, hostile land,
who guarded vulnerable crosswalks
of dangerous Baghdad streets.

INEQUALITY

On the tormented Earth,
battered by disrupted Nature,
assaulted by every form, type
of man-created destruction,
it may be too late for harmony
between tenants and landlord.

The well-meaning have become smarter,
more concerned with matters of survival,
making themselves custodians
for preservation of habitation.
But arrayed against conservers
are legions of darkness,
who obey their masters,
corrupted servants of the greedy
who consume our tomorrows
in unregulated indulgence,
threatening continuation.

Children die of AIDS in Africa
because profit won't allow treatment,
Asian children are sold into bondage
for sexual gratification of the wealthy.
Children in the Mideast
are seduced by relentless fanatics
into the select sect of suiciders.

Across this tortured globe
good is overwhelmed by evil,
contrived by the indifferent
against the defenseless,
leaving us diminishing hope
that miracles may rescue us.

American Intervals

When the New World was first settled
common people constructed
the illusion of freedom,
encouraged by their masters
lusting to pluck
tantalizing fruits of a continent
ripe for exploitation.

Soon settlers grew tired of constraints,
moved west, until they ran out of west
and were lured to opportunities
in burgeoning cities,
promising relief
from feudal toil of farming.

Then another revolution
spawned the machine age,
static serfdom for its workers
who banded together
against mechanized oppression.

For a while it seemed
that humble toilers could compel
begrudging overseers of power
to share benefits of effort.

But share is alien to oligarchs,
whose only mantra is more,
who took their riches elsewhere
and only paid a pittance
to undemanding foreigners,
abandoning former workers to rust
in decaying cities of industry.

The Long View

Short-term tenants
on the indifferent Earth
greedily grubbed their way
to accumulation,
first survival weapons,
spears, fire, meat, furs, fuel,
primitive requirements
necessary to insure
desired continuation.

The exercise of power
won storage space
in caves of comfort,
allowing distribution
in varied times of need,
or for public rewards
of vital commodities
for services rendered
by loyal followers.

The innovation of cities
provided greater space
for storing more goods,
permitting more resources,
regardless of weather,
or enemy siege,

to sustain a household,
personal bodyguards,
constabulary, armies,
until one controlled many.

This is history's lesson,
briefly contradicted
by illusions of democracy.

Elegy to The Child Soldier

Recruited by brutal abusers
too callous to care about them,
children are brainwashed to commit
dreadful crimes against humanity,
as terrible as those afflicted
on the innocent children themselves.

The first condition to convert
children into deadly weapons
is a failed state that can't protect
children from being abducted,
or enticed by opportunists
to enlist in warring armies.

How easily children's minds
are altered by ruthless warlords,
who don't allow refusal,
promise an end to hunger,
protection from harm by magic,
the comfort of belonging.

Once in the grip of warlords,
the merely vicious bandits
plundering a troubled land,
there is no escape until death,
except for the fortunate few
who manage survival.

And the horrors they see
forever blemishes them,
until immune to pity
they carry out massacres,
unimaginable bloodbaths
the form of hygiene practiced.

In the still protected USA
we are shocked at a child killer
and cannot conceive of children
burning other children alive,
pounding babies to death in mortars,
as if they were grinding grain.

Children are exploited
by cruel thugs and criminals,
and automatic rifles
become toys for child's play.
Suddenly a twelve-year-old
is a dangerous weapon.

When Iran issued plastic keys
to open the gates of heaven
for thirteen-year-old children
who cleared Iraqi minefields
by sacrificing their bodies,
there were no outraged protests.

When warlords teach child soldiers
life and death depends on spirits
conjured up by their commanders,
distilled in oil and amulets,
children do unspeakable things,
moved by supernatural fears.

When the world finally noticed
terrible atrocities
the U.N. passed a protocol
that combatants must be eighteen,
but neglected to provide
means of enforcement.

DO WE GET WHAT WE PAY FOR?

Once political office
attracted honest men
ambitions forgiven,
since ambition isn't a crime.
By the twentieth century
motives of office seekers
were questionable.

When women entered politics
we had a fleeting hope
they'd be more honest than men,
but hope was fleeting.

Now that elective office
is purchasable
for large sums of money,
a seat in the U.S. Senate
costs sixty million dollars.
A White House seat
costs considerably more.
Sometimes we know who pays the bill.
Generally, we don't.

Like it or not,
our future is for sale
to the highest bidder.

Bombs Bursting in Iraq

The biggest killers in Iraq
that murdered American troops
were powerful roadside bombs,
considered responsible
for four of five combat deaths
in a struggle against chaos.

Yet at home politicians claimed
it wasn't their fault we're fighting there,
President Bush should be blamed.

To some the war was a mistake.
Others thought it was proper.
It matters not who's right or wrong
when our sons and daughters are dying.

Despite our fears we won the war
with incredible efficiency,
a minimum of casualties.
Our problems began
when we were ill-equipped
to win the peace.

History will or will not answer
the questions about our decision
to disband the Iraqi army,

to purge Sunnis from the government,
to neglect to establish order
when the opportunity was there . . .
And other multiple mistakes.

But our politicians
criticized the war,
the same war they voted for,
and demanded we bring troops home
and weren't really concerned
that improvised explosive devices
were the biggest killers of our troops,
and didn't make urgent demands
to develop new devices
to protect our threatened soldiers
who were fighting in Iraq.

IRAQ DILEMMA

Political opponents
of the administration
invoked the ghosts of Vietnam
that still haunted the nation,
though many tried to forget,
and raise specters of defeat
for our venture in Iraq.

Granted that it was foolish
to make war in the Mid-East
without a clear-cut mission,
a pacification plan,
an exit strategy,
but why blame our president
when congress voted for war,
our people endorsed the war,
except for foolish dissidents
easily dismissed.

So we were in a quagmire
that was nothing like Vietnam,
but still consumed our soldiers
and still devoured our treasure.
Then former war supporters
loudly demanded
withdrawal of our troops,

or else they'd cut off the funds
for our soldier's plane fare home.

The lords of industry
made sufficient profit
selling war equipment
and were kindly listening
to clamors for retreat.
They accepted a cease fire
as soon as it was practical
and soon discovered
the horror we unleashed.

Biofuel Confusion

Gas emissions choke the world.
Ministers of greed chortle
as profits sustain their power,
letting them ignore perils
that fossil fuel is creating
for poor and privileged alike.
Oppressive regimes are sustained,
their people bought or suppressed
in a world oil dependant,
making Earth more polluted.
Oil profits cushion our masters,
support our enemies,
pay for weaponry,
fund plots against civilization.

We are trapped in oil servitude,
manipulated to consume
what the lords of profit decide
until the haves become sated,
while have-nots simmer in anger.
Yet leaders of the USA
ignore the problems of fossil fuel
and accept the poisoning
of air, earth, water, our future,
while means of survival
become obliterated,

and we are oblivious
to wanton destruction
of our children's tomorrows.

The tyranny of oil decrees
higher speeds on highways,
higher prices for fuel,
larger vessels for shipment,
longer pipelines for transport,
regulated production
for economic control
that determines consumption,
which insures dependency
on a diminishing resource
that may do more good than harm,
but punishes us for usage
that we only seem to protest
when prices go up at the pump.

Our leaders propose
alternative energy,
presenting various options
from silly to futile.
One recent popular choice
is corn-produced ethanol
that eager advocates assert
will replace costly, toxic oil.
Greedy farmers rush to plant
bigger and bigger corn fields,

planting fewer and fewer crops
that feed animals and man,
so everything will cost more,
while animals and man will eat less.

Corn is a row crop
that adds to soil erosion,
contributes to pollution,
needs tons of fertilizer,
huge amounts of pesticides,
expends large amounts of fuel
to grow, harvest, and dry,
which causes nitrogen runoff
that consumes vital oxygen.
This alternative fuel
makes almost as much greenhouse gas
as the gasoline it replaces
further depleting the soil,
competing with food production.

Some leaders wave the banner of green
claiming corn-produced ethanol
an alternative to fossil fuel,
but that is merely illusion.
Our energy dependency
on diminishing fossil fuels
threatens the world's food supply
as farmers plant less
wheat, rice, peas, rye, other crops,

increasing the price of grain
that feeds our livestock, poultry, us.
In the pursuit of more profit
more acreage will be used for corn,
further depleting the food chain.

If the entire U.S. corn crop
was used to produce ethanol,
it would only replace twelve percent
of U.S. gas consumption,
lead to rising prices
for processed and staple foods,
affect the relationships
of food producers, consumers,
all nations of the world,
threaten global poverty,
threaten food security
in the global food system,
slightly annoying the haves,
further distressing the have-nots.

Using gasoline and ethanol
is burning a candle at both ends
consuming itself wastefully
in our endless lust for energy.
Windbags urge wind or solar power
that cannot answer our demands
for more and reliable power.
When fossil fuel is exhausted

and ethanol depletes the earth
and the wind no longer blows
and the sun no longer shines,
we're left with few alternatives
except nuclear energy,
or huddling in caves again.

Running Interference

Fulminations at government
are rarely appreciated
by elected officials,
except when authorities
need a convenient distraction
from accusations of wrongdoing.
Then media deceivers
solemnly oblige our leaders
reporting local corruption,
reporting horrible murders,
by reporting lurid trials,
until we no longer remember
our justifiable suspicions.

Depredation

The works of man
are smothering our planet,
suffocating the surface
with coats of concrete
denying respiration.

Toxins pollute the land,
poison the air,
sterilize the seas.

Those who care,
hoping our children
will have a future,
bravely raise their voices
but are stifled
by confusing clamor
broadcasted daily
by the servants of profit
to distract us from danger.

Reality Check

Literally believing
in constitutional rights
of life, liberty, the pursuit of . . . ,
is a violation of
intelligent observation,
as well as common sense,
since liberty is eroding
for honest citizens
making life more dangerous.

When the Founding Fathers
wrote noble words
they may or may not
have believed them,
but they inspired
the insecure public.

In an age of limited vision
the internet allows
democratic expression,
so every fool will have his say,
at least where it's allowed,
and we are deceived
with electronic illusions
into blindly believing
we're exercising freedom.

Questions of War

In ancient wars
generals led from the front,
compelled to face the foe
to set an example
for apprehensive troops
who soon would confront
axmen and spearmen
eager to drink their blood.

Gunpowder changed warfare,
bringing death from afar,
beyond reach of the sword,
which had made war personal.
Generals moved behind the lines
to survive longer,
but still were close enough
to direct the battle.

Long-range artillery
and far ranging aircraft
made generals decide
to move further to the rear,
safe from intrusive bombs
that interfered with planning.

Once generals felt secure
they quickly got comfortable,
sheltered from perils of the field,
ordered better food and drink
than was provided to the soldiers
fighting in the trenches,
and began to forget the creed
to always lead by example
and soon were detached
from daily threats to the troops.

Yet American families
didn't understand
why a general's life
was worth more than a soldier's
who was much closer to danger,
and entrusted their children
to reassuring leaders
who avoided the question
of whose lives were more precious,
experienced combat troops,
or rear-echelon generals.

Role Reversals

Corridors of power
once led to organized
government installations
that issued commands from
White House, Pentagon, Kremlin,
moving or shaking the world
now made almost impotent
by corridors that may lead
to wood shacks, mud huts, caves.

The Democratic System

We besiege the middle class
with crime, drugs, taxes,
dangling the prizes of consumerism
slightly out of reach,
and raise the cost
of elective office
so the government
of the, for the, by the people
is managed by the wealthy,
or compliant vassals
who orate virtuously
serving the oligarchs,
as the American dream crumbles.

Rules of Engagement

Foreign affairs
mean different things
to various classes
in democratic America.
To the educated,
relations with other countries
are the only possibility.
Business schemers
hungrily visualize
Eastern European women,
bought and paid for
like any commodity.
A small percentage of escapists
and a much smaller group
of speculative scientists
imagine alien encounters,
benevolent or hostile.
What is most reassuring
to our self-appointed rulers
is that the mass of our citizens
have been conditioned
to only engage in fleeting pleasures.

Danger Sign

In a conflicted world
that produces
seething nationalism,
rabid terror,
the overwhelming need
for preservation of species
is easily forgotten
by temporal rulers,
besotted with appetites
that urge them to consume
the diminishing fruits
of the devolving earth.

Desertion, or Treason?

Once when our country still made things
in the heyday of World War II,
lots of our workers were happy
and harbored secret fantasies
of becoming millionaires.
Granted they never believed it,
but they hoped their kids would get rich
and until globalization
their offspring still had a chance.

After our jobs and capital
kissed the USA goodbye,
because it cost too much at home
to make a sufficient profit
for those who never made enough
and only wanted to make more,
the solution was quite simple,
go where everything is cheaper.

It cost too much to retool
the factories that could compete
with new technologies abroad
that replaced expensive labor
with automated work systems
that didn't require benefits.
So the workforce once considered

the backbone of our country
was allowed to dwindle away,
with no concern that the future
basically offered servitude
for holders of low paying jobs.

Yet some economists assert
this is a normal evolution
from a farm economy,
to factory economy,
then to service sector jobs.
Eighty percent of our workers
have been demoted to servants
with a useful side benefit,
servants rarely become strikers,
thus allowing corporations
to dictate economic turns
to the subservient people.

Now gone and never to return,
our factory jobs went to Asia,
or welcoming third world countries
eager to accept the money
pilfered from our nation's workers,
now reduced in purchase power,
forced into a lower lifestyle.

There are many moral questions
for those who live in abundance

regarding their obligations
to those who live in poverty,
but lack of ethics has prevailed
and laissez-faire is the practice.

A few earn enormous profits,
the rest struggle to survive,
often barely more secure
than peasants in the middle ages.
More than three million jobs
went abroad since 2000
and never will return,
now enriching China,
still enriching Japan,
still bringing poverty
to American shores.

It is quite obvious
that either stupidity
or surrender to greed
suborned national ideals,
permitting the powerful
to exploit everyone else.

Our system has declined
and no longer may produce
saviors who will preserve
the future of our children.

BRIEF DREAMS

In the intermittent struggle
between capital and labor
that started in the caves,
or even earlier,
the wealthy usually triumphed,
or when briefly toppled,
wangled their way
by any means necessary,
until once again they directed
the destiny of mankind.

Jacquerie, rebellion,
revolution, all resulted in masters,
new or old,
well-disguised puppets,
dancing,
as they made the people dance
to celebratory tunes
applauding riches.

Mass Communication

The horrors of each day
brought live and in color
to our receptive homes,
never lets us recover
from the shock of blood and gore,
and may not be as destructive
as the brutal ravages
of the hordes of Attila,
the hordes of Genghis Khan,
killing, raping, looting, burning,
riding on and destroying
the next town, the next tribe.
But back then it took a while
to find out what happened,
allowing us time
to digest bad news.

Cycle of Destruction

As we cover the earth
in coats of concrete,
other suffocants,
strangulants that asphyxiate,
besieged Mother Nature
strikes back
with earthquakes,
tsunamis,
hurricanes,
forces of destruction
repaying the devastations
of inventive men,
diminishing the hope
to reestablish harmony
between habitat
and dependents.

High Policy

Many governments guarantee
the purchase of biofuel crops,
if farmers stop growing food,
but the same governments
won't make guarantees
to feed the poor
as long as the wealthy
can fill their gas tanks.

The well-to-do assume
no matter world conditions
they will procure enough
to live in luxury,
while have-nots struggle
for survival.

When government sheds the burden
of caring for the needy
in first world countries,
they condemn some citizens
to live as in third world countries.

Life, liberty, and the pursuit . . .
have been legislated away
by the servants of the people.

URBAN SORROW

The light of day wearily subsides
fatigued by man's abuses.
Intruding beams from street lamps
sing illusion songs of safety.
The gleams of light from homes, offices, stores,
pretend they are guardians of the night,
protecting frightened city wayfarers
desperate for destinations,
who only recognize peril
when trapped in ambush.

Iraqi Blues

Our troops patrolled Baghdad streets
hated and feared by all,
often greeted with smiles
that soon became sniper fire.
The deadliest threat,
improvised explosive devices,
killed and maimed wary troops,
until we can only wonder
why generals and admirals
spent billions on hi-tech weapons,
yet had no protective systems
to shield vulnerable troops
while our enemies used cheap bombs
to slaughter our sons and daughters.

SERENITY

As the bombs go off
in Baghdad, Beirut, Bombay,
we should give thanks
for temporary safety
in the good old USA

Learning Experience

A system relying on rote
does not deal well with crises
requiring improvisation
for positive resolution.
A nation of sheep
tended by shepherds
who shear or slaughter
determined by market forces,
are trapped in a process
that develops conformity,
encourages compliance
to arbitrary principles
defined as education.

Harsh Reality

There is no forgiveness in nature,
except among higher orders,
which is closer to forgetting.

There is no kindness in nature,
except for higher orders,
even that is fleeting.

There is no compassion in nature,
except among the highest orders,
that is not enduring.

The struggle for survival is primal,
except among the highest orders,
defying nature's conventions.

Compliance

Peace and prosperity
is what the public wants,
what we're taught to want.
When our children go to war
on a distant, hostile shore
if it's someone else's child
and we are comfortable
the loss is easy to ignore.

SOLDIER'S PAY

It is easy to forget
casualties of war
sitting in comfort
far from danger zones.

Shortly after World War II
the nature of war changed
and was no longer considered
a national interest,
until it involved
our children and treasure.

Subsequently, the public
turned its attention elsewhere
and the land was divided
into those who cared
for the fate of the nation
and those out for themselves.

While our children bled and died
in a country far away
we squabbled over issues
of great consequence,
in unseemly spats
that convinced our loyal troops
serving on hostile shores

that they were of little value
and easily forgotten,
despite doing their duty.

Bureaucratic Priorities

The mayor of New York
proposed a five-year action plan
to end chronic homelessness,
which so far has managed
to put more families on the street,
more than ever before.
The city spends our tax money
while innocent children suffer
terrible horrors on the street
exposed to crime, violence,
and the city keeps counting
the number of homeless
instead of finding solutions
for children cruelly abandoned
by the richest city in the world.

Gifts of Man

The earth is divided
into haves and have nots.
Haves inter the land
in choking concrete coats,
ending circulation.
Have nots ignore the land,
paralyzed by fear
of desertification,
allowing strangling sand
to end hopes of life
when someday
the twain shall meet.

Ode to Automatic Weaponry

Shots fired in anger
resonate beyond
normal confines
rapidly penetrating
security barriers
designed to protect
innocent bystanders
from intruding projectiles,
too widespread to be uninvented.

Climate Change

Fertile land turns to desert,
drying up water
blighting the environment,
creating large-scale migrations
causing a global crisis,
and political instability
in Africa, Central Asia.

Immigration at home or abroad
is the only option for the poor
at risk of displacement,
by desertification.

Climate shifts add further stress
to increasing populations,
diverting rivers
for irrigation,
but they cannot store water
in the rainy season
for use in dry spells.

By 2050
billions will leave their homes,
driven out by climate change,
becoming nomads,
unwanted, threatening
unwelcoming neighbors.

GRUDGE

The world is a spectacle of having,
yet for those who have not,
deprived of participation
in fruits of the earth,
there is no consolation
in repeated promises
that never come true.
Unlike rebellions in the past
over faith or freedom,
current storms of violence,
fueled by greed, drugs, hatreds,
are further aggravated
by the daily display
of desirable goods,
only obtainable
by illicit acts.

Planned Obsolescence

Americans' peculiar ideas
have conditioned our belief
in strategic bombing,
so our leaders rant righteously
while carrying a smaller stick,
as we substitute technology
for the human element,
which allows us to accept
replacement by machines,
whose caretakers justify
remote destruction.

All the News

The constant bombardment
of disastrous news
non-stop on TV
across the world
teaches us geography,
reminding us daily
that tragedy is global,
as America leads the way
in violence innovation.
The usual methods
of time-tested brutality
are universally practiced,
but our alienated children
still manage to surprise us
with fatal rampages.

Deep Sixed

The light of day has faded. The probing eyes of street lamps emit glimmers on the walls of houses. Vast office buildings are abandoned, reminding us of our brief tenancy on the unheeding earth. Concrete crypts await us. The comforts of deception will constrict our resting places.

Brief Bereavement

The creatures of nature
do not brood long
when some are subtracted.
Short term memory
shields the ephemeral
from anguish of loss.

Beaten Down

The myths of life do not reveal
how to endure the intolerable.
When the day's affront
multiplies insolence,
we fold our hands,
nod heads in acceptance
too beaten to resist,
flee to deathly dreams
seeking immigration
to a safer climate
from real or imagined offense,
fearful of more affliction.

Ex-President

Time, whose hands
intent on strangulation
grip him, day to day,
boding illness,
birthing dread,
taunting him,
an old man
searching redemption,
remembering a young man
expecting fulfillments,
who now must mourn
the passing of power
and reluctantly succumb
to the judgment of history.

Winter of Discontent

I am a restless man
pacing the dark hallway,
exiled from the dining room
where the women play cards,
the men toil in the kitchen
mumbling consoling jokes
as they wash the dishes.

SWAN SONG

I see too many faces
bitter and shriveled
by the summer sun,
smileless masks
of drab routine
battered by obligations
humming survival's song,
the grating sound
of a submerging city.

Super Highway

The lights from cars, trucks, buses
pierce the night highway
birthing us kin a moment or two
with other estranged drivers
as we race past foreign vehicles
intent on unknown places
in a land that dispossesses us.

HARVEST

Pass us no beginnings
for tired of toys
and idle mischief
we stirred no longer.
And when the first fruits
turned to ashes
in our imploring hands
and we exhausted tears,
we were left impoverished,
defeated planters.

Overwhelmed

The infinite lassitude
palling over us,
a wave of unknown tides
crashing on our mortal remains,
disconnects us
from further service.

Vox Populi

In a world ruled by oligarchy
idealists dreamed of democracy,
shed their blood in revolutions
that evolved to internet solutions,
and provided mass communication
for the electronic generation,
who discovered to their dismay
that every dolt will have his say.

Darwinism

The loss of habitat
eradicates more
than our myopic eyes
ever notice
and the ecosystem,
once completely shattered,
will remove the food chain
that sustains
birds, beasts, man.

Attrition

Loss of purpose
frequently afflicts
those once dedicated
to righteous causes,
finally worn down
until overwhelmed
by crushing burdens
of selfish interests,
resistant to change.

American Myths

The Founding Fathers devised
E Pluribus Unum
and are considered giants
in the annals of history.
Their intellectual stature
dwarfs our current leaders,
who face a level of problems
that might have stumped
Al, Tom, Jim, Ben.

Lost Souls

Perish our tomorrows
when sinned against,
or sinning,
we sleep fleeting days away.
This sorriest creation
whimpers longings,
squanders time,
bloated citizens
couched and dreamy
clots of expectation
in danger of waiting
until our moment fades.

Shock Treatment

Old poems of love
make us dream
sweet moods,
noble thoughts,
but visions of torment
stir our fears,
stab our hearts
with lances of pain
that penetrate,
break off, fester,
leaving us deprived,
spiritually naked.

URBAN EXPANSION

Soon half the world's population
will live in towns and cities,
abandoning agriculture,
at least until World War III.
Natural increases
and migration of the rural poor
to towns and cities
swamp government services,
creating enormous slums
where people live in shanties
without water, sanitation, power,
unable to improve conditions.
The victims of neglect
pollute urban watersheds
with untreated sewage
and contribute to the rise
of crime and violence,
while denied opportunity
to escape from poverty.

Deceptive Aim

Tempt us not to surrenders,
how often we have pleaded,
desire being the weakness
that admits infirmity.
The quiverings of reason,
spasms of attainment
threaten lifetimes of deception
trapping us in illusions.

SHOPPING SPREE

The frigid city
gasps for breath,
a polluted bandit,
stealing hope.
Foreign tourists
are not ethereal
and their search for sunlight
leads them hot and pregnant
to the portals of Macy's,
where they kindle transactions,
leer genuflections.

Demented Species

Omnivorous animal
impatient of arrival
moved by urgency
more imminent than hate,
lusts to consume
the entire earth.

RÉCHERCHÉ LE CHOSE PERDUE

A coy old woman
adrift in her 1920's
sack dress, flaunting beads,
bangles, bracelets,
vestiges of the past,
a glamorous female turkey
gobbling away the years,
haunting the jeering streets
searching for a cultural event
that reminds her of her youth.

Russian Visit, 1903

Into the harbour in gleaming motion
sailed upstart ships of shining steel,
glistening white in virgin splendor,
the untested battle fleet
of a nouveau arriviste nation
confronted the old world powers
with urgent appetite for a share
of exploitable wealth
of the undeveloped world,
proclaiming dramatically
that greed in a democracy
is the same as in a monarchy.

Last Chance

Before we have a great fall
from careless, greedy abuse
of our fragile eco-system
that cannot endure
endless assaults
on air, water, food supply,
there may be a chance
to regenerate Earth,
if we begin
resurrection.

The Counting of the Homeless

Instead of offering
sufficient services
to address the needs
of a vulnerable group
removed from normal haunts
of alienating society,
whether from dysfunction,
dire calamity,
fire, loss of job,
money expended
in counting the homeless
should be used
to provide shelter.

Altogether Dreamless

Master of incomprehension
cheerlessly unproductive,
adrift through office days,
barely afloat in city nights,
desires wrapped in confusion,
lost to avenues of arrival
that might provide comfort,
an isolated outpost
dwindling in vigilance,
expectations in tatters,
as remaining hungers
fracture to shreds.

You Can't Go Home Again

Hours or minutes passing
encased in soaring plane
through dark night
in unrevealing sky
suspended above Earth
bound for undesired destination
that once smashed childhood illusions,
made more distasteful
by anticipation.

No Salvation

The hand of help
I could not see
outstretched throughout my youth
may or may not have been there,
but if it was, it evaded me.
Now older, wiser,
forsaking judgment,
recriminations,
having done as much
for needy youth
as I could manage,
I can only grieve
for our lost children.

Victims of the Past

Love has few enchantments
when scrutinized too closely
by wary participants
hesitant to concede
themselves to another.
Fearful of rejection,
unallayed apprehensions
emanate from youth,
stifle a resonating cry
that painfully insures
no dream endures.

Pedestrian Traffic

How strange to watch people pass
through a tiny park in the city,
wondering who are kind,
who have time for pity
as their hard feet crunch the concrete,
feet that have trod distant lands
carrying fools and posers
to foreign shores,
then back to our shores
where they huddled together
lusting material pleasures,
scorning enlightened dreams.

Waste Not

So much for thoughtless youth
spent in fleeting moments
that we are briefly lent
to use with care,
or thrift, or not at all.
Then the swift decline
in which we fall
faster than bits of matter
hurtling through the universe,
living for a cosmic instant
before we disperse.

Munich in the Mist

Church towers with ghostly clocks
loom through haze of evening mist
like distant peaks of stolid mountains
indifferent to swirl of violence below
that often swept this conflicted land,
delivering death and destruction
with periodic relentlessness,
leaving hope of continuation.
Only the final solution
to the terrors of humanity
will sustain assurances
of spiritual yearning.

Two Dirges

I   Allurements

> We are born too late for enchantments,
> demons never seem to tempt us here,
> just crones beckoning from embankments,
> mechanically mumbling in their fear.

II   Causality

> Long before ethics and morality
> called for universal equality,
> the lust for power and basic greed
> were the main motives of human need.

SACRIFICE

I have built of my anger a pyre
and set your foolishness upon it,
I, lover, healer, tyrant.
Your fingers twitch supplications,
but unheeding
I ignite the greedy logs
bruising your nakedness.
Your body of commotion gone
I snare your escaping smoke,
bottling the sad wisps,
and live with your purest essence.

Redeemed

In the frenetic world again,
I rush a mad citizen
aping my brothers.
I move through city masses
an indistinguishable swirl
of spasmodic haste
in subway teeming,
on streets of shoving,
in shops of hurry,
once again recruited
a dweller in chaos.

GUILT

Songless tongues
quickly utter despair
at tortured times that pass
without a moment's ease
from tormenting thoughts
of what we did or did not do,
which we're destined to endure
for our remaining days.

No Forgiveness

Many young men
dream of writing,
but distracted by fantasies
of great deeds,
public acclaim,
beautiful lovers
curled upon midnight beds,
they neglect their chores.
The guilt of failure,
a grim, black panther
stalks, claws unsheathed,
listens to evening atonements,
ignores puny excuses,
punishes those
who have not struggled,
then evaporates,
a sudden mist
devouring compassion.

Three Rueful Songs

I
From the depths of self-revulsion
praise to the love of woman, praise
that we forgot in selfish days
spent in spasms of convulsions.

II
Women who have loved us in their ways
a moment or longer with sentiments
for any reason, so many days,
never getting more than fragments.

III
Too busy with tomorrows
that we fear we'll never make,
we cannot ease your sorrows
as we watch you slowly break.

FINIS

When fossil fuel is exhausted
and the forests are depleted,
we will hulk by imaginary fires,
prisoners of feeble memories,
until our last indulgences
have been extinguished.

Poems from *Fault Lines* have appeared in:

Blink Literary Magazine, Caesura (Poetry Center San Jose), *Century 21, Contemporary Literary Review India, Dark Sky Magazine, Dirty Chai, Dual Coast Magazine* (Prolific Press), *Fine Lines, Fullstop Literary Magazine, Heavy Bear, In Parenthesis, Keep Going Magazine, Literal Minded, Lotus Reader Literary Magazine, Madswirl, Matter Monthly, Montreal Serai, New Maps, Nazar Look, New Verse News, Outward Link, Over the Edge, Post Poetry Magazine, Protest Poems, Quay Journal, Record Magazine, Samizdat Literary Journal, Secret Press Anthology, Sentinel Literary Quarterly* (UK), *Shades and Reflections Magazine, Six Sentences, South Jersey Underground, The Avalon Literary Review, The Chicago Record, The Driftwood Review, The Juke Jar* (Canopic Publishing), *The Neglected Ratio, The New Verse News, The Recusant, The Redbridge Review, The Scrambler, The Stray Branch, The Transnational, Third Eye, Word Salad Poetry Magazine,* and *Workers Write* (Blue Cubicle Press).

Brief Dreams, a chapbook, which later became part of *Fault Lines*, was published by Medulla Publishing.

About the Author

Gary Beck has spent most of his adult life as a theater director, and as an art dealer when he couldn't make a living in theater. He has had numerous published works including the poetry collections *Days of Destruction*, *Expectations*, and *Dawn in Cities*, and the novels *Extreme Change*, *Flawed Connections*, and *Call to Valor*. Gary's original plays and translations of Moliere, Aristophanes, and Sophocles have been produced Off-Broadway in New York City, where he currently resides.

www.ingramcontent.com/pod-product-compliance
Lightning Source LLC
Chambersburg PA
CBHW051345040426
42453CB00007B/425